Lantern of Diogenes

written & illustrated by Tamer Dishek

Band of Brutes Publishing

www.bandofbrutes.com
www.twitter.com/bandofbrutes
www.instagram.com/bandofbrutes

Copyright © 2016 by Tamer Dishek

All rights reserved. This book or any portion thereof may not be reproduced or used in any manner whatsoever without the express written permission of the publisher except for the use of brief quotations in a book review.

First American Paperback Edition

ISBN: 0692544461

ISBN-13: 978-0-692-54446-4

Library of Congress Catalog Card Number: 2015916486

For the outliers

Introduction

This is a book of lyrical thoughts, firsthand observations, and irrepressible beasts.

T.D.
Buffalo, New York
October 24, 2015

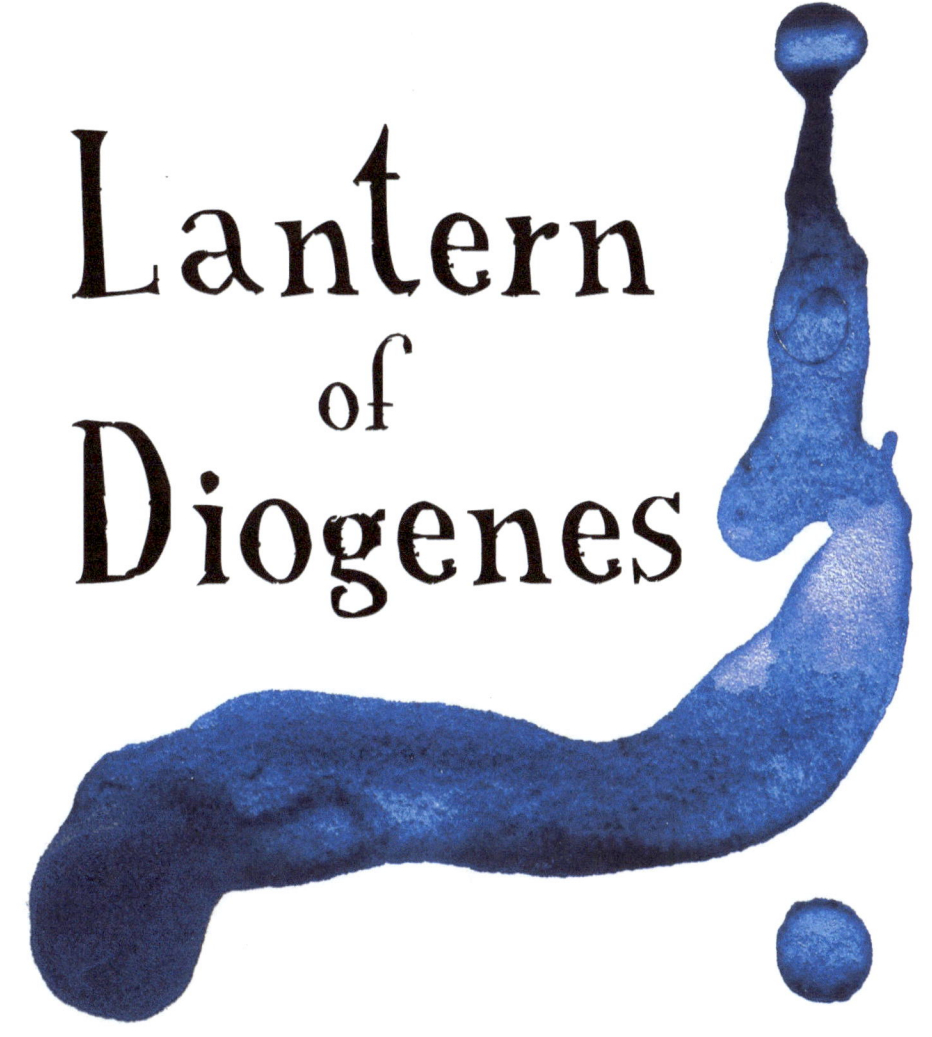

CAT

The world is
brimming with wonder.

(To the delight of all
　　　　with eyes to see.)

OVELLA

Gadflies hold a key position
in any garden of earthly delights.

(A position that grants them
some blistering views.)

SNIENGAN

Generalizations have much to say.

(Just not about individuals.)

KINYONGA

Sincerity camouflages itself
most comfortably in humor.

(Think back to the last time
someone made a joke about you.)

ZILONUS

Those quickest
to offer advice are often
those who need it the most.

(A funny quirk of nature,
let's call it.)

STRAUSS

People are a curiously irrational bunch.

(Who love using logic to deny it.)

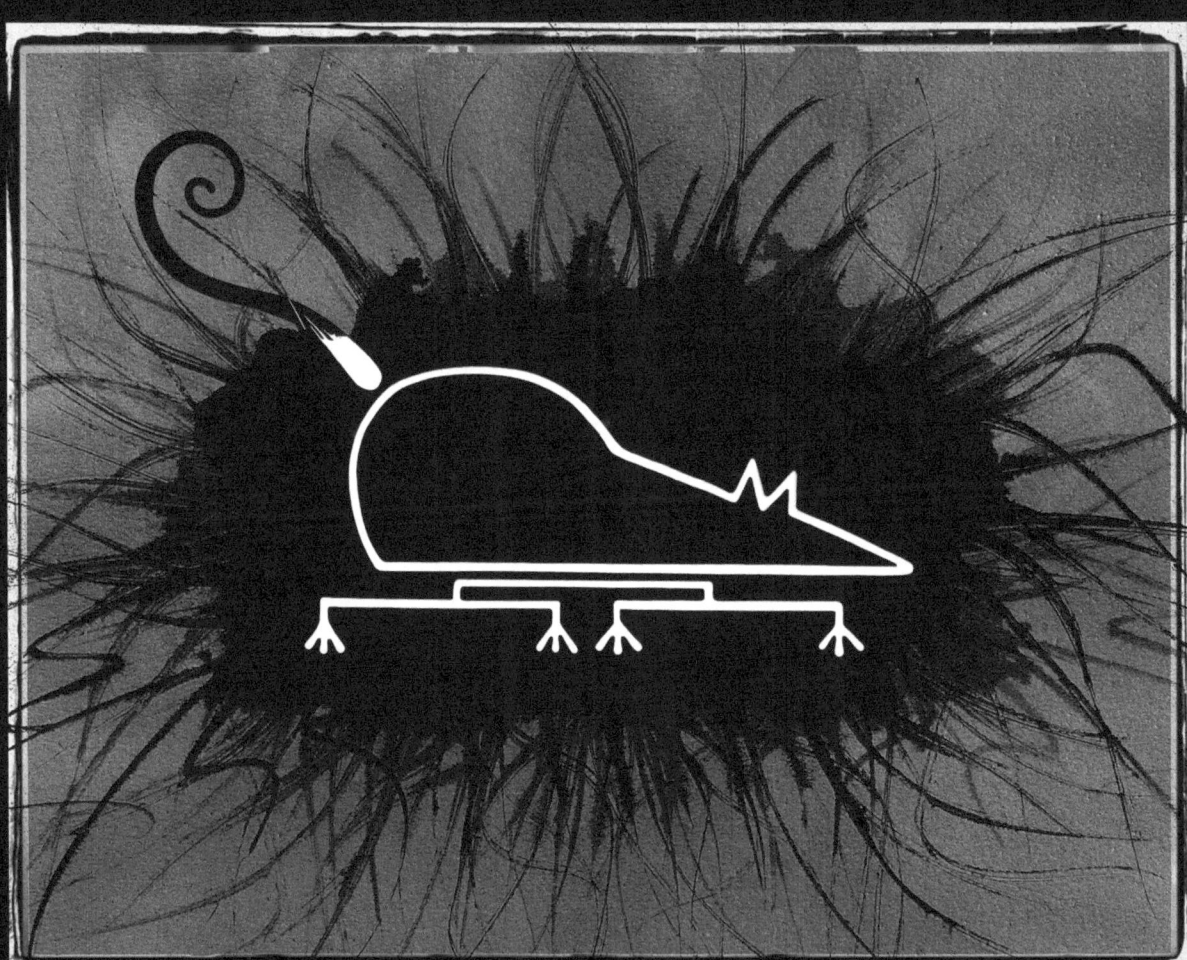

FRANCACH

A compassionate heart reminds us that bad people are not as bad as we make them out to be.

(A dispassionate mind reminds us that good people are not as good as we make them out to be.)

VOLAVKA

The world needs
thoughtfulness.

(But that's not what it wants.)

ZORRO

Life is a paradox.

(One ill-suited to the confines of a box.)

GANGURRU

Competition brings out the best in humanity.

(The best in terms of performance.)

BRANCO

Learn to trust in the validity of your own experience.

(No matter what your tribe says.)

NOSOROGA

Technology can be bought, but not the wisdom to use it.

(This is the great challenge of our times.)

WIKUNA

The loudest mouths
 are seldom the wisest.

(...)

EQUUS

Few, indeed, ever dare to follow the passion in their lives.

(A fact which family, friends, enemies, and **society** itself all find rather comforting.)

TWIGA

Love lives in a land
 riddled with pitfalls.

(The worst of which
 are known by most
  and avoided by few.)

BROGA

Deeds, not words.

(Especially in the presence
of good looks and charm.)

ASTERION

The populace of Ancient Rome was fed bread and circuses to keep it content.

(A neat trick that never seems to lose its luster.)

UCCELLO del PARADISO

Kids believe in fairy tales
just as grown-ups
believe in fairness.

(Despite all evidence
to the contrary.)

NILPFERD

The way of harmony does not mean the way of comfort.

(Of the things that are forgotten, this is one of the first.)

KRINGMERK

The prime casualty
of a throwaway culture
is the human heart.

(Make no bones about it.)

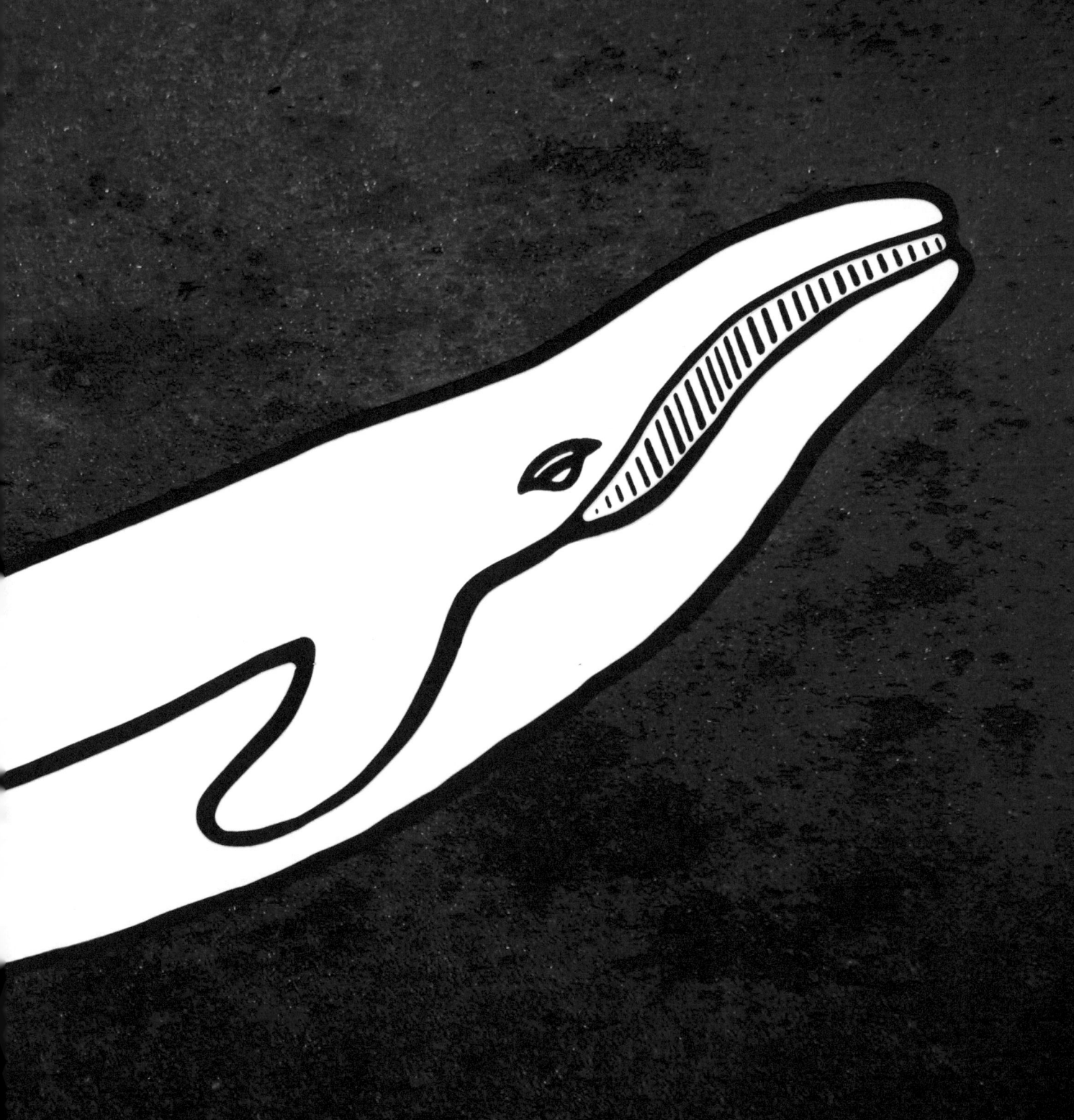

KIŠKIS

Question everything.

(If you dare.)

TORTUGA

Everyone you will ever meet is capable of teaching you something.

(About yourself, if nothing else.)

GURITA

Bias lurks in the hearts of all.

(Manifold are its manifestations.)

TUCANO

The power of perspective is a freak of nature.

(Whether it's a blessing or a curse depends on you.)

XORUZ

Find your well of ideas where you will.

(Be it in that quiet place between thoughts, or that loud place within them.)

MANDO

A hollow life is one that obsesses over the very things least likely to fill it.

(Here are some of the usual suspects: money, power, food, sex, drugs, celebrity, sports, titles, rank, fashion, entertainment, work, and all sorts of expensive junk.)

EEKHOORN

If your life isn't evolving,
then it's devolving.

(There is no such thing
as staying "the same.")

APINA

Moderation in most things.

(Most of the time.)

POISSON

Inauthenticity is a communicable disease.

(One that afflicts the young from the moment they're told to "Say cheese!")

LEOPARDO

People with a victim mindset do themselves a great disservice.

(As does anyone else who views them in that way.)

BAHAW

The game of good and evil
was created
    by mankind, for mankind.

(Don't expect anyone else to play.)

ASLAN

Consider the perks of a bigwig lifestyle:
a crown of anxieties,
    a shift of scruples,
        a question of allegiances...

(... and a table at the restaurant
of your choice.)

KONIK MORSKI

Serendipity distinguishes between those who are ready for it and those who are not.

(Or so it would seem.)

CABRA

Shortcuts are for the uninspired.

(The scenic route is where the magic happens.)

PALLUA

When you take someone for granted, you remind them of just how beautiful life can be.

(Without you around to spoil the view.)

STAG

Friendship is as rare as sunshine through rain.

(And just as welcome.)

PORUMBEL

To be human is to recognize one's shortcomings.

(And simply leave it at that.)

PILLANGÓ

A wasteland is a place crawling with imposters.

(Find one conveniently located behind your back
and right under your nose.)

MERLA

Decency.

(A lost art
if ever there was one.)

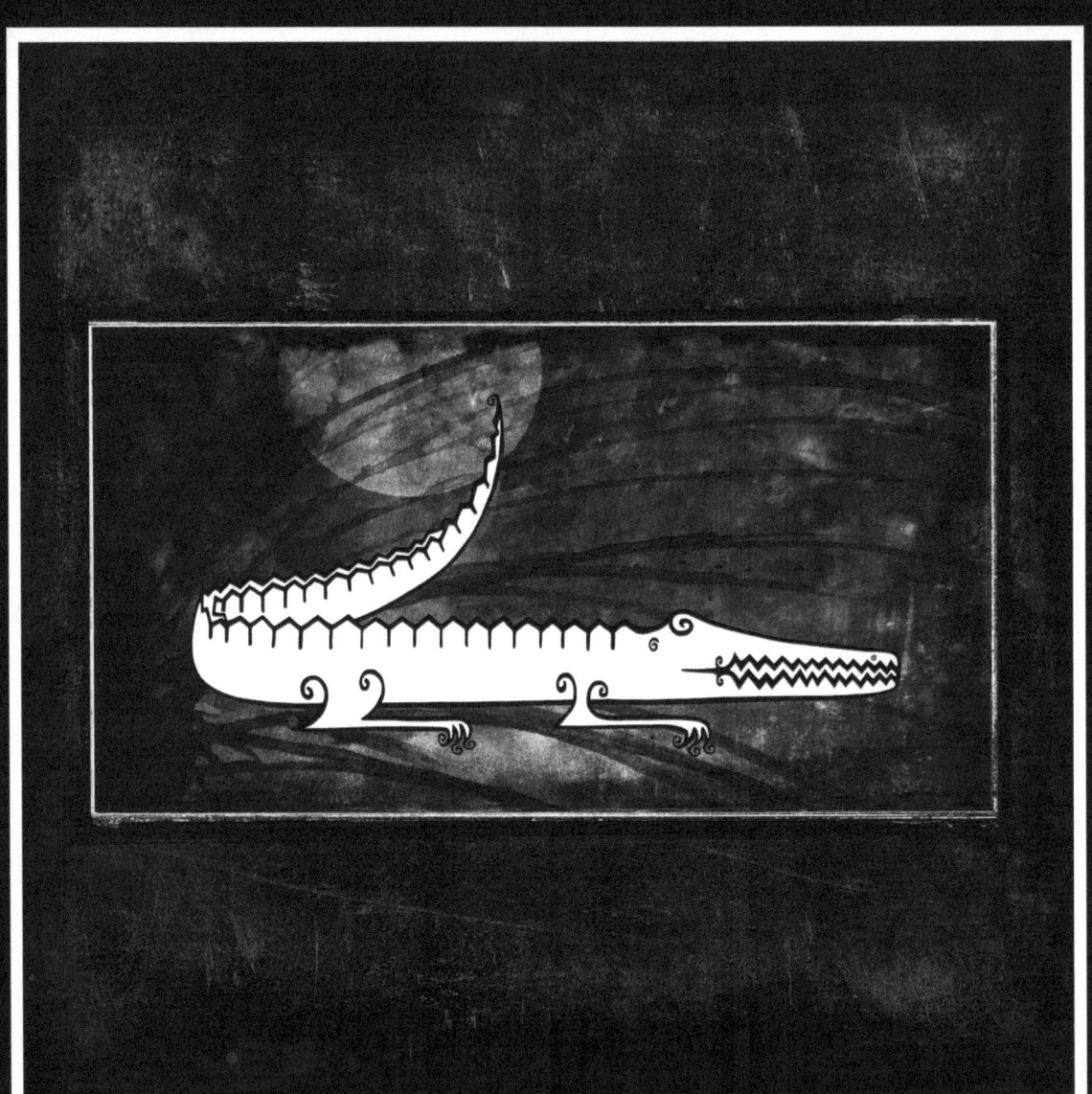

TIMSAH

Those who whisper secrets to you,
whisper secrets about you.

(In case you haven't heard.)

PINDSVIN

Today heals tomorrow.

(If given **half** the chance.)

MARA

It all begins with you.

(What are you waiting for?)

Tanglesome

www.ingramcontent.com/pod-product-compliance
Lightning Source LLC
Chambersburg PA
CBHW042005150426
43194CB00003B/136